W9-ANT-592

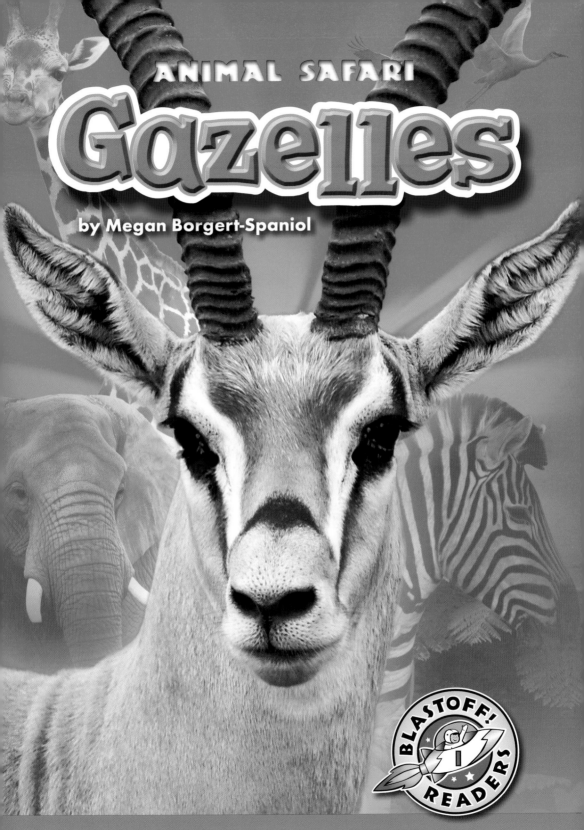

ANIMAL SAFARI

Gazelles

by Megan Borgert-Spaniol

BELLWETHER MEDIA · MINNEAPOLIS, MN

Note to Librarians, Teachers, and Parents:

Blastoff! Readers are carefully developed by literacy experts and combine standards-based content with developmentally appropriate text.

Level 1 provides the most support through repetition of high-frequency words, light text, predictable sentence patterns, and strong visual support.

Level 2 offers early readers a bit more challenge through varied simple sentences, increased text load, and less repetition of high-frequency words.

Level 3 advances early-fluent readers toward fluency through increased text and concept load, less reliance on visuals, longer sentences, and more literary language.

Level 4 builds reading stamina by providing more text per page, increased use of punctuation, greater variation in sentence patterns, and increasingly challenging vocabulary.

Level 5 encourages children to move from "learning to read" to "reading to learn" by providing even more text, varied writing styles, and less familiar topics.

Whichever book is right for your reader, Blastoff! Readers are the perfect books to build confidence and encourage a love of reading that will last a lifetime!

This edition first published in 2013 by Bellwether Media, Inc.

No part of this publication may be reproduced in whole or in part without written permission of the publisher. For information regarding permission, write to Bellwether Media, Inc., Attention: Permissions Department, 5357 Penn Avenue South, Minneapolis, MN 55419.

Library of Congress Cataloging-in-Publication Data
Borgert-Spaniol, Megan, 1989-
 Gazelles / by Megan Borgert-Spaniol.
   p. cm. – (Blastoff! readers: animal safari)
Includes bibliographical references and index.
 Summary: "Developed by literacy experts for students in kindergarten through grade three, this book introduces gazelles to young readers through leveled text and related photos"–Provided by publisher.
 ISBN 978-1-60014-768-5 (hardcover : alk. paper)
 1. Gazelles–Juvenile literature. I. Title.
 QL737.U53B68 2013
 599.64'69–dc23
                                    2011053016

Printed in the United States of America, North Mankato, MN.

Contents

What Are Gazelles?

Gazelles are **mammals** with long necks and long legs. Most gazelles have horns.

Gazelles live in dry grasslands. They gather in groups called **herds**.

Grazing

Gazelles **graze** on grasses, **shoots**, and leaves. They get water from the plants they eat.

Gazelles also stop at **watering holes** to drink.

Predators

Gazelles must look and listen for **predators** when they drink.

They use their long
legs to run from
cheetahs, lions,
and leopards.

Sometimes gazelles **pronk** as they run. This tells predators to stay away.

Fawns

Female gazelles give birth to **fawns**. Mothers hide their newborn fawns in tall grass.

Fawns run with
the herd after two
or three weeks.
Keep up, fawn!

Glossary

fawns—baby gazelles

graze—to feed on plants and grasses

herds—groups of gazelles that travel together

mammals—warm-blooded animals that have backbones and feed their young milk

predators—animals that hunt other animals for food

pronk—to jump up and down with stiff legs

shoots—stems, flower buds, or leaves that are just beginning to grow

watering holes—natural areas filled with water; animals gather at watering holes to drink.

To Learn More

AT THE LIBRARY
Doudna, Kelly. *It's a Baby Gazelle!* Edina, Minn.: ABDO, 2009.

Meinking, Mary. *Lion vs. Gazelle*. Chicago, Ill.: Raintree, 2011.

Robbins, Lynette. *Gazelles*. New York, N.Y.: PowerKids Press, 2012.

ON THE WEB
Learning more about gazelles is as easy as 1, 2, 3.

1. Go to www.factsurfer.com.

2. Enter "gazelles" into the search box.

3. Click the "Surf" button and you will see a list of related Web sites.

With factsurfer.com, finding more information is just a click away.

Index